How to Slay a Serpent

Stephen Ritchie

Presentation by BookLeaf Publishing

Web: www.bookleafpub.com

E-mail: info@bookleafpub.com

ISBN: 9789357745192

First edition 2023

ACKNOWLEDGEMENT

Thank you Ella for your contribution to this book. It would not be what it is, without your amazing work on the cover.

PREFACE

Isaiah 50:4-7

"The Sovereign Lord has given me a
well-instructed tongue,
to know the word that sustains the weary.
He wakens me morning by morning,
wakens my ear to listen like one being
instructed.
The Sovereign Lord has opened my ears;
I have not been rebellious,
I have not turned away.
I offered my back to those who beat me,
my cheeks to those who pulled out my beard;
I did not hide my face
from mocking and spitting.
Because the Sovereign Lord helps me,
I will not be disgraced.
Therefore have I set my face like flint,
and I know I will not be put to shame."

Part 1:The King Arrived

John 12:1-8
"Six days before the Passover, Jesus came to
Bethany, where Lazarus lived, whom Jesus had
raised from the dead. Here a dinner was given in
Jesus' honor. Martha served, while Lazarus was
among those reclining at the table with him.
Then Mary took about a pint of pure nard, an
expensive perfume; she poured it on Jesus' feet
and wiped his feet with her hair. And the house
was filled with the fragrance of the perfume.
But one of his disciples, Judas Iscariot, who was
later to betray him, objected, 'Why wasn't this
perfume sold and the money given to the poor?
It was worth a year's wages.' He did not say this
because he cared about the poor but because he
was a thief; as keeper of the money bag, he used
to help himself to what was put into it.

'Leave her alone,' Jesus replied. 'It was intended
that she should save this perfume for the day of
my burial. You will always have the poor among
you, but you will not always have me.' "

Climax of History
He's in charge of funds, the money, the fees

He was on the heel of the King for years.

He follows the Law to the "T".
He's "perfect", God's teacher, holy.

But she's a sinner, her past left her worn,
But what she has she pours out on His feet.
At their glances of scorn,
She was ready to hang her head in defeat.
Until she is reassured by Christ's Words:
Her story will be told throughout the world.

The pit is dug, the trap is set.
The scheme to slay the serpent
Has been put into motion,
Because they believe He's a threat.
All the pieces are in place on the board,
They're going for the King, The Lord.

Not willing to change or repent
These are the villains, unwilling to let go,
So they slayed and lifted the serpent.
These are the ones history won't forget
Not because they were the heroes,
But because they lived for the Hero, no regret.

He's the governor of the land,
And he's washing blood off his hands.

He's a master of torture, the head of a rigid
regimen.
He crucified the man, after called Him the Son
of Man.

He's just a passerby,
But he's aiding the man condemned to die.
He's modeling how to carry your cross,
Before millions will go on to live it out,
How to live selflessly and consider the cost.
He's being drafted into history being written out.

Christ has breathed his last,
And the die has been cast.
The curtain is torn, laid in the dust,
And the spear has been thrust.
He asks why His own Father has forsaken him,
And the chalice has been poured out, full of
earth's sin.

Not willing to change or repent
These are the villains, unwilling to let go,
So they slayed and lifted the serpent.
These are the ones history won't forget
Not because they were the heroes,
But because they lived for the Hero, no regret.

Triumphant Entry

He is on a colt, not a stallion,
And they are shouting praises, laying palms.
Crowds urge the holy king to carry on,
While the teachers try to get them to be calm.

He is David's blessed descendant
And their hero ready to conquer Rome.
At his response, they are left indignant,
But Jesus rides to give outcasts a home.

He was born, and laid in a manger,
And now he now leads a band of misfits.
He has no home, but calls home the stranger,
Whether fisherman, drunkard or Zealot.

He loves like Father running to the prodigal,
And the righteous brother finds it too radical.

John 12:12-15, 19
"The next day the great crowd that had come for
the festival heard that Jesus was on his way to
Jerusalem. They took palm branches and went
out to meet him, shouting,

 'Hosanna!'

'Blessed is he who comes in the name of the
Lord!'

'Blessed is the king of Israel!'

Jesus found a young donkey and sat on it, as it is
written:

'Do not be afraid, Daughter Zion;
see, your king is coming,
seated on a donkey's colt.' ...
So the Pharisees said to one another, 'See this is
getting us nowhere. Look how the whole world
has gone after him!' "

Battle Hymn

He's the God who formed the mountains like
clay,
Arrayed in light brighter than break of day.
At His voice winds and waves of the storm
cease.
Surrender is the way, the path to peace.

When He speaks, it sounds like booming
thunder
And His lightning shreds the sky asunder.
He leads forth constellations, like the Bear,
And mans the post which the winds are sent here
or there.

He pulls the Leviathan by a hook
And knows our days, all written in His book.
He gives the owl wisdom, strength to the horse.
He guides the sun as it runs its whole course.

In wonder His enemies bow.
For they see the Mighty King now.
So fly a banner in His name,
For with no other does He share His fame.
March in step with His right decrees,
Or you will be counted with those who flee.

The God who named and breathed out every
star,
Joined the battle to take what should have been
our scars.
He's our commander; obey each order.
Draw strength from His love, good Christian
soldier.

When the pain is fierce, do not lose your hope.
Be the strong few who go against the flow.
Because the end of this war, we already know,
Even when the tension is taut like strung out
rope.

Our praise is roaring with power,
Love is restoring us in our darkest hour.
In wonder, our enemies bow,
For they see our Mighty King now.

This is my anthem, it's my battle hymn,
My song to remember and honor Him.
While I'm still fighting on earth in this war,
My courage and confidence remain sure.

Where the border splits the lands, I'll belt out
this song.
With my sword in hand, my melody will play
on.

His Righteous my rhythm, my heart beats
In harmony with His. Come on now, no retreat!

Sweat pouring in rivulets down my face,
I lift my eyes to heaven's grace.
I am exhausted, panting from the fight
But I find my hope knowing His burden is light.

Our praise is roaring with power.
His love's restoring us in our darkest hour.
His pealing thunder is like our drum roll.
His resurrecting power fills my soul
Like lightning coursing through my veins in the
fighting.
In wonder my enemies bow,
For they see my Mighty King now.

Luke 19:38-40
" 'Blessed is the king who comes in the name of
the Lord!'

'Peace in heaven and glory in the highest!'

Some of the Pharisees in the crowd said to Jesus,
'Teacher, rebuke your disciples!'

'I tell you," he replied, "if they keep quiet, the
stones will cry out.' "

Cry Out

Molech and his zealots are alive and well.
They claim it's about freedom,
But they are in bondage to the practices of Hell.
The old tradition of child sacrifice never left,
It was only reinvented to leave the mother
bereft.

They drown out God's voice by their
wickedness,
For a lie, they gave up truth and righteousness.
They call for a sustainable solution,
While pumping the youth's hearts full of
pollution.

No one pleads the case for the just,
No statement is made with integrity.
Their arguments don't hold enough weight to be
discussed.
They conceive trouble and birth iniquity.

They hatch viper's eggs to fill their nest,
And spin the webs spiders weave.
They invite guests and give poisoned eggs to
ingest.

And their cobwebs decorate their sinewy
sleeves.

Justice is far from us,
Where do we have to go?
Righteousness will not reach us.
We look for the light,
But walk in the shadows.
Truth is nowhere to be found.
Honesty is barred outside of town.
The just are driven back.
Whoever shuns evil
Falls prey to attack.

Even with my back against the wall,
I will resolve to consume no corruption at all.
If I remain silent now, I will perish,
But God's deliverance will still arrive.
God chose this time for each of us to be alive.
So we will choose to praise and cherish
Our Heavenly Father and King.
The days are dark, yet we will still sing.
We will speak, and raise the shout,
Because if we don't, these stones will cry out.

In the streets they make lengthy prayers,
But never lift a finger to help the load people
bear.

By their exchanges, they made this house of
prayer,
Into a den where the thieves dump out bounty to
share.

They are a brood of vipers and white-washed
tombs.
They are the renowned slayers of the prophets.
They preach in order to fill the room
And teach to line their pockets with profit.

They traded the truth and reality,
For false promises and prosperity.
Travel the world for one convert, only to make
him twice the son of Hell.
Sow $35 in faith, and you will be happy, healthy,
and well.

The time has come when people won't tolerate
sound doctrine.
Instead they will follow their desires and sin,
And seek teachers who speak out what their
itching ears
Long to hear. They chase fleeting fantasies in the
mirror.

Justice is far from us,
Where do we have to go?
Righteousness will not reach us.

We look for the light,
But walk in the shadows.
Truth is nowhere to be found.
Honesty is barred outside of town.
The just are driven back.
Whoever shuns evil
Falls prey to attack.

Even outnumbered, I will keep my head in each
situation.
I will endure as an evangelist, proclaiming
salvation.
I will pour myself out as a drink offering,
Until I lay my crown at the feet of the King.
I will not slow down, until I finish my race,
And see my Savior face to face.
I will speak the truth and be consistent.
I will step out and not be silent.
Because if I ever try to tap out,
The moment I do, these stones will cry out.

Luke 19:45-46
"When Jesus entered the temple courts, he began
to drive out those who were selling. 'It is
written,' he said to them, 'My house will be a
house of prayer; but you have made it 'a den of
robbers.'"

The Hummingbird and the Sparrow

A dazzling hummingbird drifts down on a
flower,
Wings aflutter as he hovers for nectar.

A sparrow exits her chirping nest,
Winging out not for herself but for
The hungry mouths that will rarely let her rest.

He leaves as soon as he has had his fill,
Always moving, never content to be still.

She returns with food for her wanting young,
And comforts them until they are content and
still.
This sparrow serves even when it is less than
fun.

He can go forward, backwards, and hover
Side-to-side, but never to help another.

Finally, she nudges to the edge each chick,
They drop, but then soar, thanks to their mother.
Loving each one, that is her niche.

To all the handsome and haughty out there,
Even flowers are gifted in Solomon's wear.

And God sees and blesses even the sparrow,
Because He strengthens the weak, where
He also humbles the proud. Just know,

Dazzling hummingbird, who lives for getting
more,
There's more to life than your sweet nectar.

Luke 20:45-47
"While all the people were listening, Jesus said
to his disciples, 'Beware of the teachers of the
law. They like to walk around in flowing robes
and love to be greeted with respect in the
marketplaces and have the most important seats
in the synagogues and the places of honor at
banquets. They devour widows' houses and for a
show make lengthy prayers. These men will be
punished most severely.' "

God of the Valleys

God, you called me to the mountain
And though the climb was tough, You showed
me majestic views.
I saw the kingdoms of the world.
I learned to apply your word.

Like the Mount of Transfiguration,
I saw you like never before.
I lived each day, burning bright
Like Elijah on Mount Carmel
I prayed for fire, and I Am sent it down.

Now I have descended the mountain,
And I am abiding with the Lord in the valley.
It takes longer for sunrise to break over the ridge
And I have no clue what may lie ahead.

But my God has dominion over the mountain
And He rules in the valley.
He can be victorious through us
In the high and in the low.
Our God is the God of the Valley.

Now the enemy has started crying out, saying

"Yes, the Lord gave you victory on the
mountain,
But your God only has power over the
mountains.
I will have victory over you in the valley
Because your God is a god of the mountain
But not a god of the valley."

At the enemy's call
I recall the last time I descended into the valley.
How depression set in.
How I used the time to rest and recover,
But in my heart I was still camped on the
mountain,
When work was needing to be done in the
valley.
Satan won't let me easily forget
How the mountain fell on me.

God, help me believe you have dominion over
the valley.
Remind me You can be victorious through me
In both the high and the low.
You are my God even in the valley.

God, send your wind into this valley.
Breathe new life into my soul,
Raising a warrior from dry bones.
Stoke a passion that springs from the waiting,

Like the anointing at Pentecost.
Victory shall be claimed in the valley,
Because you are the God of the Mountain,
And the God of the Valley.

Ballad of Bethal

Among the Dreamers, the heroes, I roam.
We're adventurers who never leave home.
We who pledge hand over heart to grandeur,
But we don't dare to step out the front door.

On our journeys, we have seen sights untold,
Only accessible through imagination.
If only we could grow to be more bold,
We could conjure up any creation.

If we could hurdle our hesitation,
And remove our reservations.

Another dreamer, was hoping, fleeing
Just to escape there with his life.
Longed for the first rights, but ended in strife.
Now desert stars were all he was seeing.

At Bethel, he was dreaming that night,
Of stairs teeming with angels in bright light.
God gave a dream, a promise at Bethel.
And though Israel still would one day wrestle,

Jacob still believed God would follow through.
Jacob would more than just survive,

He would even flourish and thrive.
Not just family, but a nation, too.

Jacob had not the comfort of a bed,
But God gave him a dream instead.

If our thoughts never flow into our hands,
Disaster will leave revival in sand.
People are lacking, without our innovation,
Because we are slacking, dry on motivation.

We could supply them with every solution,
Bless them each with exotic vacations,
But we pass up every chance for resolution.
We have been called, but take up no
convocation.

We could share and invite them to lands that
excite,
But not if we bury our ingenious insight.

Another dreamer, he was tattling,
But he already lived the dream.
God desired a river from a stream,
And for Joseph to soar on wind and wing.

Joseph was faithful in that foreign land,
But in Egypt, God set forth a wise plan.
When he dreamed how his family would bow,

He knew not of the journey that led him to now.

He would more than live, but save many lives
Become the king of many, not just survive.
From betrayed, to a slave, to a dark cell
To everything restored and ending well.

We have the visions, but we doubt.
Why do we not believe God could carry it out?
He could make dreams into reality.
But we instead forfeit eternity.

As we sleep a little longer,
The darkness grows ever stronger.
The true hope is in our hearts and our heads,
But we will not even roll out of bed.

We long for the ring of the chains breaking,
And the knees of tyrants quaking,
But instead we decide to wait.
We want victory and to celebrate,

Until it requires work to participate,
It takes a toll to become someone great.

God made our souls for stellar dreams,
We trade His fellowship, for our own gain it
seems.
He will place new desires in our hearts,

He will ignite fires, if we'll let Him start.

With mustard seed faith he will move
mountains,
With obedience, spring desert fountains.

It is here at Bethel, God gives us dreams.
Where the great gates of heaven open wide,
May we choose to let his Spirit inside.
His permanent home, not just a hotel.

It is here at Hebron, God gives us dreams,
When we were complacent and just content,
We learned, something better, was His intent.
When the journey is long, may we dream on.

Matthew 23:37-39
" 'O Jerusalem, Jerusalem, the city that kills the
prophets and stones those who are sent to it!
How often would I have gathered your children
together as a hen gathers her brood under her
wings, and you were not willing! See, your
house is left to you desolate. For I tell you, you
will not see me again, until you say, 'Blessed is
he who comes in the name of the Lord.' "

Broken Cisterns

I brought you into a fertile land
To eat its bounty and rich fruit.
But you defiled my land in which you took root.
And made my inheritance too evil to stand.
Those who dealt with the law did not know me;
The prophets foretold by Baal,
Following worthless idols' empty thrall.
The leaders rebelled against me.

Has a nation ever changed its gods or its king?
But my people have exchanged their glorious
Lord
For worthless idols and wicked things.
Look what they have forsaken me for!
The spring of living water and their Father,
For broken cisterns that cannot hold water.

God's well of life and living water,
Why would anyone exchange for another?
With hearts like cracked cisterns,
Idols and sin will leave you no water.

If you knew of God's great gift
And who it is who asks you for a drink,
Then you would know and you would think
To ask for living water, flowing swift.

Everyone who drinks this water will be thirsty
again
But like a mouth always open to steady rain.
Whoever drinks the water I give will never
thirst.
It will be a spring in them which fills until it
bursts.

Idols and sin will leave you empty.
Like salt water that leaves you thirsty,
The ways of the world are unworthy,
Don't trade them for God's glory.

It's like God brought us to the Promised Land,
But we got too comfortable and forgot to make a
stand
Against evil. We settled for the bounty and the
fruit,
But forgot the God in whom we anchor and take
root.

If we remembered God's great gift,
Then we would be on revival's brink.
Why do we doubt and why do we think

God is not enough? Then sin leaves a rift.

God's well of life and living water,
Why would anyone exchange for another?
With hearts like cracked cisterns,
Idols and sin will leave you no water.
Like salt water that leaves you thirsty,
The ways of the world are unworthy,
Don't trade them for God's glory.

Luke 19:47-48, Luke 20:26
"Every day he was teaching at the temple. But
the chief priests, the teachers of the law and the
leaders among the people were trying to kill
him. Yet they could not find any way to do it,
because all the people hung on his words."

"They were unable to trap him in what he had
said there in public. And astonished by his
answer, they became silent."

The Words I Wield

I set out on a quest on the page,
To dig deep into truth piled through the ages.
Not sure where I would go, or what I would
find,
It took commitment and time.
This is what I returned with, after many an hour
I found words to wield, infused with power.
You claim you have words, too,
And yeah, you kinda do.

But tell me, do your words cut through bone and
marrow
Dividing through both heart and soul?
As you puzzle over why your words are blunt
arrows
Fired at stone walls, while mine are wrecking
balls,
Leveling strongholds, I'll whisper how it's
possible,
"These words are truth, so they stand through it
all."
I extend a cure, undefiled and pure.
It's salvation, the road to a future.

Until words spill from your lips, which before
you contained,
You won't be able to leave the enemy slain.
It is a long process, agonizing and pained.
Yet, here I stand and behold what I gained:
Truth can be so close, so get on it!
Dig deep to check if you are standing upon it.
In order to fly over others, know the
conventions.
Soar by means of your own invention.

Sometimes we write and words fall,
Come running only to hit a brick wall.
Know the walls, so you can shatter it all.
Step into the wardrobe; follow Narnia's call.
Embrace the narrative's increasing friction,
And though your stories are fiction,
They become fact, because truth they don't lack.
Load your arsenal, so you're ready for the
attack.

Faith in His Word is your shield
Know the truth, and when you do, you will
wield
Your words like swords, clashing against the
lies.
With belief and confidence, your limit's the sky.

Then when you stand in the imaginary, the
fantastical scene,
You have a hope beyond fact, a hope in the not
yet seen.

Broken Record Player

This is the only track on the record,
In order to hear again, I would record.
If any other song was stuck in my head,
I would probably wish to be dead,
But if the record skips on this one song,
I will forever and always sing along.

The song about God coming down from above,
The part about the strength of his unending love.
The chorus about him wanting to be the light in
me,
I could vibe to that for eternity.

If my music was stuck on rewind,
And stuck on this one song,
I would not even mind.
I would not care how long,
It will encourage and remind
Me of truths I need to hear,
And its melody will ease my every fear.
This is music to my heart,
So why not repeat and repeat
The most important part.

Well, the record skipping, is getting the best of
me.
It does start to drive you crazy.
When "Jesus Loves You" was sung since I was
five
Until this hour I am alive,
You start to feel as if you have gotten enough.
You want variety. The monotony gets tough.

I want a jukebox, I'll insert a token.
Just don't give me that same Christian song.
I'm done with the player being broken.
Yeah, of that timeless truth, it's good to remind
But I feel like I need to get out of here.
Yes, even though His Word relieves my fear.
Hmm, maybe this resentment is actually poison
to my heart,
The commonplace of the Gospel, might drive
God and me apart.

The Gospel is a mystery no matter how well
known.
I have to recall it's a sea that goes ever deeper,
And a mountain climb ever higher and steeper.
It's an uncharted land, the end of which is never
shown.
Like a lover inventing new ways to pour out His
heart,

God's love for me when we first met, was only
the start.

It's a cup overflowing, a story worth retelling,
My greatest possession that I'm never selling.
His love is a journey with the unseen.
A movie with details you never realized before.
It is not what it first seemed
It's what you always dreamed for and more.

John 12:30-36
"Jesus answered, 'This voice has come for your
sake, not mine. Now is the judgment of this
world; now will the ruler of this world be cast
out. And I, when I am lifted up from the earth,
will draw all people to myself.' He said this to
show by what kind of death he was going to die.
So the crowd answered him, 'We have heard
from the Law that the Christ remains forever.
How can you say that the Son of Man must be
lifted up? Who is this Son of Man?' So Jesus
said to them, 'The light is among you for a little
while longer. Walk while you have the light, lest
darkness overtake you. The one who walks in
the darkness does not know where he is going.
While you have the light, believe in the light,
that you may become sons of light.' "

Déjà Vu

You called me onward,
And I assumed it was a straight shot forward.
Life would be a train on a one-way track,
Full-steam ahead, no turning back.

Everything was provided in the wasteland,
And every enemy was delivered into my hand.
The storm came, but I walked the waves.
It seemed like all of life's mishaps,
Would fall into line and behave.

I reached the summit victorious.
I thought my every venture would be glorious,
But I didn't have enough faith for the Promised
Land.
I learned to watch my successes fall like sand,
Shifted through my empty hands.

I'm back in the wilderness,
Stuck in my doubts and questions.
My heart and my soul are a mess.
I can't believe I'm reliving the same situations.
Sheesh, it sometimes feels like Groundhog's
Day.
When I'm freaking out in the tempest,

Why can't I remember how you made a way?
While I panic, you're at rest.
I'm confused by this deja vu,
But God, it is no mystery to you.

Then I put my head down,
I tried to obey a little harder,
Be the new man in town.
All for you, God, go a little farther.
I just had to train harder to beat the Enemy,
Be more disciplined, so from my sin I could
break free.
I tried a different path to reach the top of the
mountain,
Because I didn't want that desert valley again.

But I'm back. I might as well get used to this.
Derailed again by sin and life's busyness.
I'm wrestling with my doubts and questions,
And fighting hard in the same situations.
Hey! I've seen this before! Call it deja vu.
God, what do you want me to do?

What I forget, is the desert was a planned phase.
I leaned on You more, back in those days.
In the storm you're my anchor.
When I don't have all the answers,
My trust in Your wisdom is more sure.
You teach me new lessons,

From my same questions,
And my recurring doubts.
These round two's are what You use.
For each time I repent,
And every morning, your mercies are new.
Each time I'm knocked down,
You'll help me rise to beat the Enemy again.
This isn't just a phase,
It's the season you have me in.
I'm thankful for the deja vu.

Luke 22:1-6
"Now the Feast of Unleavened Bread drew near,
which is called the Passover. And the chief
priests and the scribes were seeking how to put
him to death, for they feared the people.
Then Satan entered into Judas called Iscariot,
who was of the number of the twelve. He went
away and conferred with the chief priests and
officers how he might betray him to them. And
they were glad, and agreed to give him money.
So he consented and sought an opportunity to
betray him to them in the absence of a crowd."

Part 2: The King Betrayed
Mount of Olives

Betrayed by blood and forced to flee
By fate, By God's will, king by destiny.
By judgment, now a refugee.

Cursed and afflicted but not forgotten.
Suffering, mourning in exile
Yet David's still faithful all the while.

He forgives the offense, looking ahead
Believing God will turn it to good instead.
Weeping the warrior ascends, with covered head
Barefoot trods the Mount to which this journey
led.

This is the Mount of Olives.
Where the king endures his son's rejection.
This is Gethsemane,
Where olives are crushed.
It's here where this righteous ruler
Is being crushed under the weight of the world.
Though he's weeping, he's submitting to God's
will.
Though his life is bared to suffering,
And his soul to God's reproach,

He will be faithful still.
There will be no resistance.
The Lion turned lamb will be silent
When he descends the Mount of Olives.

Betrayed by a friend's familiar kiss.
For silver, their past was all dismissed.
Before time began, He was destined to be King.
By judgment, now a criminal facing reckoning.

Cursed and afflicted but not forgotten,
Suffering for every Jew and Gentile,
To the end, He will follow through,
And be faithful all the while.

Death in exchange for the forgiveness of every
offense
He will endure it for the joy set before him.
The disciples follow, after singing a hymn.
With washed feet, they tread the Mount
To which this whole journey led.

This is the Mount of Olives,
Where the anointed King will face death before
his resurrection.
This is Gethsemane,
Where olives are crushed.
The Righteous One is crushed under the weight
Of the sins of the world.

Though he's sweating blood, he submits to
death.
Though his body is bared to suffering
And his soul to the Father's reproach,
His love did not hold back anything.
There is no resistance
When the Lion of Judah is silent
Like a lamb before the shearers.
When they leave him at the Mount of Olives.

Betrayed by friends and family, forced to flee,
Named, "crowned one", one day it will be.
By judgment, deserved wrath and agony.

Burdened and afflicted, but never forgotten.
There's suffering, I'm not in denial.
Yet God is still faithful all the while.

God, help me to forgive each offense,
Looking ahead, believing you will turn it to
good instead.
Even weeping, I will still ascend, with my
bowed head,
And barefoot trod the Mount to which my
journey has led.

This is my Mount of Olives,
Where I will learn to endure rejection.
This is Gethsemane,

Where dreams are crushed.
Here and now, my faith is tested,
As I am crushed by the weight on the world.
Though my life is bared to suffering,
I know my soul will never bear your reproach.
So I will carry on.
There will be no resistance.
When I could boast or rage like a lion,
I will be still and gentle like a lamb,
When I return to life and descend this Mount of
Olives.

Luke 22:39-44
"Jesus went out of the city to the Mount of
Olives as he usually did. His disciples followed
him. When he arrived, he said to them, 'Pray that
you won't be tempted.'

Then he withdrew from them about a stone's
throw, knelt down, and prayed, 'Father, if it is
your will, take this cup of suffering away from
me. However, your will must be done, not mine.'

Then an angel from heaven appeared to him and
gave him strength. So he prayed very hard in
anguish. His sweat became like drops of blood
falling to the ground."

Mosaic

Father, I thank-you for them.
They each brought and offered something
Unique, beautiful and wonderful.
Your Word says they are your workmanship,
Your masterpiece in the making.
They are being chiseled like a statue,
Revised like a poem,
Until they will finally be the creation you
desired they would become.

They are a mosaic. They are a stained glass
window.
A mosaic that depicts your story of redemption.
You shined through them in a rainbow array,
When they walked in kindness, truth, and love
More and more each day.
They came together to make this mosaic,
As they taught, as they danced, as they sang,
As they performed, as they witnessed.

It seems like a tragedy to crack the mosaic,
Or shatter the window.
Each of them you will fit into a larger mosaic.
An essential piece in a new mosaic, a
A new role in an even larger cast.

Their painted shards you will graft
Into an even greater masterpiece.

So God, I pray you will go before them and
behind them.
Lay your hand of protection upon them.
There is nowhere they can go from your
presence.
They are fearfully and wonderfully made.
Your thoughts toward them outnumber
The grains of sand in the desert.

I ask that you give them the Spirit of wisdom,
So that they may know you and your will better.
May their eyes and hearts be enlightened
So they may know the hope to which they have
been called,
Which is the glorious richness of your
inheritance.
It is the inheritance given to your holy people.
Give them your incomparably great power,
Given to those who believe.
The power you give them is the same
That raised Christ from the dead.
So give them strength in your Spirit.
Let them see you can do infinitely more,
Than they could ever dream or imagine.

I have been faithful to remind them of these
lessons.
Though even before I stepped into their lives,
They were firmly established in truth.
It was right of me to refresh their memory
As long as they were with me.
I have made every effort to see after their
departure,
They will always be able to remember these
things.
Through your Spirit, remind them of what they
have learned.

Holy Father, protect them by the power of your
name,
So that they may be one as you and your Son are
one.
I have given them your word and the world hates
them,
For they are not of this world anymore.
My prayer is not that you take them out of the
world,
Or even shield them from all the hurt it may
bring them,
But that you protect them from the Evil One.
They are not of the world.

Sanctify them by the truth, your Word.
You are sending them out into the world.

May they be one and united in you,
So that the world will know they are your
disciples.
They were my students for a time,
But they are your disciples forever.
Lord, I pray you bless and keep them,
May your face shine upon them
Be gracious to them,
Turn your face toward them
And give them peace.
Amen

John 17:13-19
" 'I am coming to you now, but I say these things
while I am still in the world, so that they may
have the full measure of my joy within them. I
have given them your word and the world has
hated them, for they are not of the world any
more than I am of the world. My prayer is not
that you take them out of the world but that you
protect them from the evil one. They are not of
the world, even as I am not of it. Sanctify them
by the truth; your word is truth. As you sent me
into the world, I have sent them into the world.
For them I sanctify myself, that they too may be
truly sanctified.' "

Rival Star

It had fallen from heaven, the Day Star,
His love of self, his own image did mar.
The Rival Star, called the Son of the Dawn.
He was the signet of true perfection,
He was blessed with a divine complexion.
Even higher he resolved to climb on
Decided to rise above, through the air
The Rival Star from in his heart declared,
"I will be enthroned on the mount on high
On the mount of assembly in the north
Ascend past the heights of the stars God called."
But from heaven the Son saw the star fall
Like a white lightning bolt from the night sky,
Like a meteor colliding with earth.

His pride filled his heart once very tender.
Wisdom corrupted from love of splendor.
Tragic end of his exquisite beauty.
He was arrayed in every precious stone,
Glossy emerald, turquoise, and red ruby.
Before the star was banished from his home.
Cherubim arrayed in satiny sapphire
Walked up and down through the stones of fire.
Blameless, but that was long before Eden,
Beautiful and wise before the Garden.

The Rival Star was cast down to the ground
A spectacle to all the rulers crowned
The Star imploded in midfall, crashes
Consumed by his own fire, to ashes.

Now another rival star has risen,
Guiding the wise men to the perfect Light.
The Light fulfilling prophetic visions,
Challenging the hold of the silent night.
Now Herod the tyrant king is shaking.
To the angels the shepherds are waking.
He came to fulfill the hopes and the fears,
And prophecies awaited through the years,
There is no more gloom for those in distress,
Beyond the Jordan, by Way of the Sea
The people who once walked in deep darkness
Now dawns a great Light to set them all free.
To us, a child is born, a son given.
For us, a chance to turn, be forgiven.

In the Light, the night long spent will soon cease
The Bright and Morning Star we now will see.
Wonderful Counselor, Mighty God, He'll be
Everlasting Father, and Prince of Peace.
He will reign on his Father David's throne
And rule over his kingdom with no end.
His reign he will uphold forevermore.
Watch sovereign deity to us descend,
The Light of the World had come to his own

Every longing soul has come to adore.
The new Adam made manifest has come
The curse laid in the garden is undone.
He'll establish justice and righteousness
The brilliance of the Son has come to us.

Among the seven gold-laden lampstands
Eyes as fire, over his chest a gold sash
Hair white as snow, Behold The Son of Man!
Skin like bronze, voice like a waterfall's crash.
Out of his mouth a double-edged sword,
His face, the brilliance of the son, The Word.
He is the Living One, The First and Last,
Who speaks with the sound of a trumpet blast.
Holding the keys to Hades and to Sheol
To the victorious, obeying soul
From God will receive the Bright Morning Star,
Worthy is the Lamb, giver of new birth
Who bought with blood, each nation near and far
Made them a royal priesthood on the earth.

In the sky, a dragon wore seven crowns
Who swept down a third of the stars by its tail.
The first rider's bow was bent on renown.
War rode like red fire, famine held the scales
And the last horse pale, as Death who rode him.
The Earth's kings gathered at Armageddon.
At Heaven's gates stood the fifth stallion white
With his rider, Faithful and True, to fight.

To fight the armies in the final war.
The Morning Stars, locked in confrontation
The two Lions clashed for all creation.
Satan was cast into the lake of fire.
There was no more crying or pain or night,
No need of the sun, The Lord is their Light.

Luke 22:50-55
"And one of them struck the servant of the high
priest, cutting off his right ear.

But Jesus answered, 'No more of this!' And he
touched the man's ear and healed him.

Then Jesus said to the chief priests, the officers
of the temple guard, and the elders, who had
come for him, 'Am I leading a rebellion, that you
have come with swords and clubs? Every day I
was with you in the temple courts, and you did
not lay a hand on me. But this is your
hour—when darkness reigns.'

Then seizing him, they led him away and took
him into the house of the high priest. Peter
followed at a distance. And when some there
had kindled a fire in the middle of the courtyard
and had sat down together, Peter sat down with
them."

To Set Apart

I come here, looking like I'm ready to give my
heart,
But it's not a destination; it's just a landmark.
I can come bringing incense to this altar,
But back at home, I practically live at another.

I come laying down my soul, but I keep back a
part,
My own little slice that can keep in the dark.
I could bring it to light, each time I falter,
But instead I choose to remain undercover.

There's a God who has loved me from the start,
A Light who came even though the world was so
dark.
His sacrifice the course of history would alter.
To call a people to Himself, he would die and
suffer.

I was made for a higher calling, to be set apart,
To be different, within the void, a spark.

He endured the hand's stinging smart,
And their ridicule as a mocked monarch.

He came to the world He created, He came to
His own.
Rejected, by those who should have made Him a
king at home.

As He gave up His spirit, the temple curtain was
torn apart.
He finished the journey from which Heaven he
left to embark.
So, God, rule again in my heart. Reclaim your
throne.
You went to such length, so help me be faithful,
no matter how much I roam.

From the dawn of Creation this was your heart,
To call a royal priesthood, sealed with Your
mark.
To this end, you pressed on that night all alone.
The Jews handed You to be killed by men of
Rome.

Kneeling, weeping at the cross, I'm ready to be
set apart.
Make me a star in the night, in the void, a spark.

Mark 14:55-65
"The chief priests and the whole Sanhedrin were
looking for evidence against Jesus so that they

could put him to death, but they did not find any. Many testified falsely against him, but their statements did not agree.

Then some stood up and gave this false testimony against him: 'We heard him say, 'I will destroy this temple made with human hands and in three days will build another, not made with hands.' Yet even then their testimony did not agree.

Then the high priest stood up before them and asked Jesus, 'Are you not going to answer? What is this testimony that these men are bringing against you?' But Jesus remained silent and gave no answer.

Again the high priest asked him, 'Are you the Messiah, the Son of the Blessed One?'

'I am,' said Jesus. 'And you will see the Son of Man sitting at the right hand of the Mighty One and coming on the clouds of heaven.'

The high priest tore his clothes. 'Why do we need any more witnesses?' he asked. 'You have heard the blasphemy. What do you think?'

They all condemned him as worthy of death.
Then some began to spit at him; they
blindfolded him, struck him with their fists, and
said, 'Prophesy!' And the guards took him and
beat him."

The Cross

The cross, a paradox of necessity,
Hangs by the front door.
It is of no logical value.
I lift the cross off the wall.
I turn it over and over in my hands.
My fingers gather dust
And ants who had built a nest inside,
Now scurry over the course, wood surface.

I hardly notice this cross, most of the time.
I need it though.
I would never dream of giving it up.
Like air, always present,
Always necessary, never remembered.

This ornament is a long-lost memory.
Rarely does it ever replay in my mind,
Yet it would tug at my heart strings,
Like a game of tug-o-war,
If it ever reentered my conscience.

This cross holds sentimental value for me,
Not for where it has been and what it has seen.
For me, it is only a reminder of the story
Of a greater Cross.

Two thousand years ago, that Roman Cross
Held not its usual wretched criminal,
But the guiltless Lamb of God, mocked, beaten,
And marred beyond recognition.
Three days later, his silhouette was encased
In a glorious, triumphant sunrise.

So the cross, a paradox of necessity,
Hangs by the front door.
In one way it is of no logical value,
But priceless in another way.

A king would never march his troops
Out to war without a coat of arms.
Declaring what kingdom the enemy dared to
challenge.
His victory is not at stake, but his glory.

A five-year-old girl could go to sleep with only a
bed,
But without her teddy bear, she would refuse.

The American flag waves for the sake of
patriots,
Citizens who know they are free and free indeed.

In the same way,
The cross still hangs there
Only for what it means for me,

A citizen who knows he is free indeed.
I could fall asleep without the cross
But I refuse.
Not for my victory,
But for His glory.

Years later, the cross now hangs above my bed,
Though I've moved several times, I still have
and display it.
It was what I wrote my first poem about.
Now that poem is being published with many
others
In this very book.

The Cross is still the anthem of my battle hymn.
The song that plays round and round in my head
Like a broken record player.
His love and forgiveness are still my fortress.

John 18:33-37
Pilate then went back inside the palace,
summoned Jesus and asked him, "Are you the
king of the Jews?'

"Is that your own idea,' Jesus asked, 'or did
others talk to you about me?'

'Am I a Jew?' Pilate replied. 'Your own people
and chief priests handed you over to me. What is
it you have done?'

Jesus said, 'My kingdom is not of this world. If it
were, my servants would fight to prevent my
arrest by the Jewish leaders. But now my
kingdom is from another place.'

'You are a king, then!' said Pilate.

Jesus answered, 'You say that I am a king. In
fact, the reason I was born and came into the
world is to testify to the truth. Everyone on the
side of truth listens to me.' "

John 19:1-6
"Then Pilate took Jesus and had him flogged.
The soldiers twisted together a crown of thorns
and put it on his head. They clothed him in a
purple robe and went up to him again and again,
saying, 'Hail, king of the Jews!' And they
slapped him in the face.

Once more Pilate came out and said to the Jews
gathered there, "Look, I am bringing him out to
you to let you know that I find no basis for a
charge against him.' When Jesus came out

wearing the crown of thorns and the purple robe,
Pilate said to them, 'Here is the man!'

As soon as the chief priests and their officials
saw him, they shouted, 'Crucify! Crucify!'

But Pilate answered, 'You take him and crucify
him. As for me, I find no basis for a charge
against him.

Luke 23:32-40

"Two other men, both criminals, were also led
out with him to be executed. When they came to
the place called the Skull, they crucified him
there, along with the criminals—one on his
right, the other on his left. Jesus said, 'Father,
forgive them, for they do not know what they are
doing.' And they divided up his clothes by
casting lots.

The people stood watching, and the rulers even
sneered at him. They said, 'He saved others; let
him save himself if he is God's Messiah, the
Chosen One.'

The soldiers also came up and mocked him.
They offered him wine vinegar and said, 'If you
are the king of the Jews, save yourself.'

There was a written notice above him, which
read: this is the King of the Jews.

One of the criminals who hung there hurled
insults at him: 'Aren't you the Messiah? Save
yourself and us!'

But the other criminal rebuked him. 'Don't you
fear God,' he said, 'since you are under the same
sentence?' "

To Slay a Serpent

Venom coursed through their veins,
Many of them passed to lay in a desert grave.
How can the venom be reversed?
How can you undo a serpent's curse?
To ease the pain, you need to kneel.
This plague came from sin, so repent,
And lift your eyes to the bronze serpent.
Do this in faith, and you will be saved.
This is how a serpent's venom heals.

Divinity coursed through His veins,
He was tested in the desert for forty days.
How can the tempter's hissing whisper be
ignored?
How can sin be overcome and victory secured?
To evade the pain, you need to kneel,
Bow your will to the King who reigns.
In mastery of God's Holy Word,
Wielded like a flashing sword.
This is how victory over the serpent is sealed.

Blood poured out from His veins,
And He was buried in the garden grave for three
days.
How can the serpent's curse be reversed?

How can humanity be set back on course?
Despite the pain, He gave His life to seal the
deal.
In the sacrifice of the Incarnate Word,
And the lifting up of the Son was the only way.
This was the way to slay the serpent,
And gain forgiveness, the chance to repent.
This was for the wounds of the nations to heal.

John 19:28-30
"Later, knowing that everything had now been
finished, and so that Scripture would be fulfilled,
Jesus said, 'I am thirsty.' A jar of wine vinegar
was there, so they soaked a sponge in it, put the
sponge on a stalk of the hyssop plant, and lifted
it to Jesus' lips. When he had received the drink,
Jesus said, 'It is finished.' With that, he bowed
his head and gave up his spirit."

Part 3: The King Alive
Silence Is...

Silence can be ugly or beautiful,
It can leave you empty or full.
When God speaks out of the silence,
It is a lion's roar.
The oppressed were silent through the violence,
But now weeping breaks the stillness of the
night,
The firstborns did not live to see another dawn
of light.
After so long, the Messiah they were longing
for.
Silence is contemplation before the solution.
Breaking silence starts a revolution.

Silence is a break from the noise and bustle,
It is the empty space, the lost piece from the
puzzle.
Silence is a chance to exist outside the rushed
routine.
It is rare, hard to come by, not often seen.
Like following a pirate's map, silence is a
treasure.
Blessed are those who seek it.
Silence is a desire, but no way to speak it.

Waiting in quiet, (silence is the anticipation)
For the sun to rise over the lake or at the
seashore.
Silence is the rest, is a musical composition,
The period at the end of the sentence.
And, it is the comma, the everything left unsaid.
Silence is the overwhelming sense of absence,
It's when you read between the lines,
And discover what's never been read.

Silence is the selah in the Psalms
There we are told to be quiet, be still, be calm.
To know He is God is the start
Of wisdom. In the silence, we give the Lord
An opportunity to speak to our hearts,
Give Him a chance to minister through His
Word.
When we don't hear from God for a long time,
When our prayers go unanswered,
And we are tested and refined.
In silence we learn how better to worship,
Besides, silence is a part of any mature
relationship.

Silence is a space to think…
To dream..
To imagine…
To learn…
To read…
To write…
To listen…
Silence is a refuge, a way in the day of distress
To escape from the chaos like it's a fortress.

Some say silence is the antithesis of sound,
But rather voice and language dance all around.
But silence is also a dark void,
An evil which many just avoid.
Silence is the lack of a voice,
And it's the refusal to make a choice.
Silence is oppression and slavery,
But in order to ease the mood,
Remember it's the sound when the food
Is good and oh so savory.

Silence is the loss of a loved one,
But also the relief when the day is said and done.
Silence is the loss of what could have been said,
Or when you bite your tongue, and stay quiet
instead.
Silence is a lost opportunity,
And when the relationship has lost all unity.
Silence is a friend who is distant,

And you long and long for them to be here.
The good news is, silence is never permanent.
Silence is the sin, when we lock up our message,
The world is dying to hear.
Silence is the meditation of the old sage,
Silence as a virtue grows in old age.
Silence is nothing left to say,
Death is the final silence on our last day.

But eternal life is imposed silence erased.
Silence is the posture of the Lamb,
And in heaven, we will see him face to face.
Silence is the martyr's death,
Believing through their sacrifice God can
Restore and multiply all that they left.
Because they refused to be silent,
Now they celebrate their victory.
Though their end on earth was violent.
Silence is the blissful "The End" of the story.

Answered

My neighbor finished building his mansion today.
Today, I just laid the first brick of my foundation.
He built his in paradise, right next to the sea.
Mine had to be built on barren, mountain heights.

So I cried out to God in frustration,
"Why can't I live in ease and luxury?"
God answered, "In this house you'll build every brick tight,
I love you, Son, but it won't be finished in a day."

So I continued building until my walls were waist high.
Then the wind blew harder, and the sky turned gray.
Torrents and lightning threatened with annihilation,
But the flood did not wash away my foundation.

So I asked God, how He could do this to me?
To have the rain come before my roof was done, didn't seem right.

God answered by pointing to the ruins of the
mansion, "That's why.
I love you Son, aren't you glad you did not build
by the sea?"

Then the walls were getting high; I was on my
way,
Until a rockslide came bringing decimation.
While the foundation stood, most of my walls
fell on me.
God, wny am I cursed here on these barren
mountain heights!

God answered, "Your neighbor, who saw, started
building today.
He just laid the first brick of his foundation.
Your reward will be in paradise, beside the
crystal sea,
Because your testimony was strong, on the
mountain heights.

Luke 23:42-49
"Then he said, 'Jesus, remember me when you
come into your kingdom.'

Jesus answered him, 'Truly I tell you, today you
will be with me in paradise.'

It was now about noon, and darkness came over the whole land until three in the afternoon, for the sun stopped shining. And the curtain of the temple was torn in two. Jesus called out with a loud voice, 'Father, into your hands I commit my spirit.' When he had said this, he breathed his last.

The centurion, seeing what had happened, praised God and said, 'Surely this was a righteous man.' When all the people who had gathered to witness this sight saw what took place, they beat their breasts and went away. But all those who knew him, including the women who had followed him from Galilee, stood at a distance, watching these things."

Renaissance

I awake to the world whizzing by
Out the window.
Sleeping on the rails isn't kind to a guy,
So I groggily peer out at the graying sky.
The world horizon erupts in a vibrant glow,
The world is repainted, gradual and slow.
Though it's hard to leave the past I know
Returning to my future is right, even though
It's hard, leaving my friends and saying bye.

We have to die before we can live again.
This is a revival.
This is the renaissance.
Die, so you can be born again.

I'm grateful for last night's sunset.
It was necessary, for the sun to rise again,
So that I may awaken to glory.
Each morning, His mercies are new,
It's another chance, a reset.
So be grateful for sunsets, for you will gain
More in the dawn, than you missed in the dark.
One chapter has to end, to carry on the story.
As hard as it is, let go of all we hold on to,
To awaken to glory, to have another start.

We have to die before we can live again.
This is a revival.
This is the renaissance.
Die, so you can be born again.

It's in the night, in the waiting,
Where gratitude and hope are hard to find.
When new is coming, and the old is gone,
Between the end and beginning.
When our hands are empty, who we are is
defined.
When we get the courage to stop hanging on,
The air bound moment flying off the trapeze
swing
When you let go of the past, yet to grasp the
future.
And in those terrifying seconds, you have
nothing.
All you lost, is yet to yield what you exchanged
it for.

We have to die before we can live again.
This is a revival.
This is the renaissance.
Die, so you can be born again.

Through the seasons of life, death births change.
Dormant trees bloom beautiful in the spring.
Birds migrate back and sing,

And we are grateful for the sound.
A seed must fall, and be buried in the ground
To sprout, flourish and bring life.
A caterpillar leaves all food and light,
For the darkness and mundane things,
In order to break free, spread its wings,
And fly. Out of the dark, it emerged, changed.

We have to die before we can live again.
This is a revival.
This is the renaissance.
Die, so you can be born again.

I will be on the tracks again soon,
Happier and singing a better tune.
The time spent in suspense was long,
But the reward came from carrying on.
While life is good, I have not fully arrived.
But I'm seeing how dying makes you more alive.
When I return to stand
In that same station,
I can say I better understand
What it means to be a new creation.

Matthew 27:62-66

"The next day, the one after Preparation Day, the chief priests and the Pharisees went to Pilate. 'Sir,' they said, 'we remember that while he was still alive that deceiver said, 'After three days I will rise again.' So give the order for the tomb to be made secure until the third day. Otherwise, his disciples may come and steal the body and tell the people that he has been raised from the dead. This last deception will be worse than the first.'

'Take a guard,' Pilate answered. 'Go, make the tomb as secure as you know how.' So they went and made the tomb secure by putting a seal on the stone and posting the guard."

Forgiveness Fugue

Lost yet to be found,
Trapped without an escape,
My debt was piled high,
My trespasses reached to the sky.

Until here on this hallowed ground,
I found the perfect goat to be my scape.
The door swung wide, my soul was freed to
race,
The whole of my fines have been erased.

Like a bird from a cage,
I am freed from bitterness and rage.
My debt piled high now is paid.
My sin that reached the sky,
Oh how much it weighed!
The burden has been lifted,
My guilt has been shifted,
And new righteousness gifted.
I have been saved today.
I am a bird flown away.

You're lost. You'll never be found.
You profess faith, but still fall in sin. You're
trapped. No escape. You think your ledger is
clear,

Just because a man died back two thousand
years?

You thought you buried the old man in the
ground. But he's still around. He leads you
astray,
And then you are in yet another scrape.
When the door swung wide, you used grace to
race, To all this world had to offer.
How are you now claiming your fines are
erased?

You'll always be a prisoner in a cage,
A slave to my accusations and rage,
Until your body in the grave is laid.
Sure! Pray to your God in the sky!
Don't bother! Don't submit yourself to shame
and degradation. Make excuses, try to get your
guilt shifted,
But I assure you this burden can't be lifted.
Why press on another day?
Hope, like a bird, has flown far away.

My heart broke at the sound
Of my friend's betrayal.
I gathered all the evidence I found
So for their crimes they could stand trial.

Until I remember that hallowed ground,
And how I was forgiven for it all.
For the door to swing wide, and my soul to be
free, I need to think back and recall
The forgiveness that was extended to me.

Like a bird from a cage,
I am lifting off, flying away,
And freeing myself from bitterness and rage. My
debt was piled high, yet it was paid.
So though his sin reached to the sky,
I will forgive his sin, no matter how much it
weighed. My burdensome bitterness is lifted,
Now that my forgiveness and mercy have been
gifted. I've been set free today.
As I have been forgiven,
I will forgive the same way.

Can't you hear it echo? The sound
Of your heart shattering at the betrayal?
Get the evidence! Stand your ground!
For their crimes! Make them stand trial!

Remember how the pain made you crumble to
the ground.

Yes, and when I was on my knees,
I was right where I needed to be.

No, now you listen to me.
Once vengeance is loosed,
And its appetite is moistened,
From its grip it is near impossible to break free.

Remaining in unforgiveness is like being
poisoned. So why would I remain caged
When I am holding the key?
Stomp, seethe, and rage,
But I'm making the choice to break free.

And another thing, Christ is my everything.
He is my salvation. My faith is in Him, not my
lack of sin. He who began a good work in me,
will bring it to completion. While I am still
fighting the old man, I am still a new creation.

Heroes Never Die

What makes a hero?
Strength, bravery, loyalty?
A drive for fame?
A desire for glory?

Those who serve without pay,
And others who are willing to give all they have
away.
Their devotion to others is certain,
Even when it's done backstage, behind the
curtain. Even if it costs them everything,
They press on, because it's done in the eyes of
the King.

These true heroes never die.
No matter how hard the world may try
To break their spirits,
They can only ever kill their bodies.
Even still their fire burns in their souls.
Their faith, hope, and love
Live on forever.
As their new bodies march into eternity.

What makes a saint?
Prayers, kneeling, and hymns?
A religious consistency

Piety, perfection, and their synonyms?

For each man imprisoned,
Another chance for change is envisioned.
For every martyr's engraved name,
It's just another billow to the flame
Of a wildfire rising higher
Than the funeral pyre.
It's those who lay their lives on the altar,
Not that they may never sin or falter.
Their witness rings true
As the darkness snuffs them out,
Like Samson's outstretched arms
On the pillars and his final shout.

What makes a king?
Is it a conqueror mounted
On a white stallion?
Israel hoped for a liberator from Rome,
A general to lead a battalion.

He came for each soul imprisoned,
But the world He created
Condemned Him to die.
He endured for the hope
He and His Father envisioned.
On that night darkness tried
To end the Light,
But instead it the fulfilled

Rescue for every soul.

The serpent had thought he won,
Until on the third day,
Rose the Son.
Christ defeated death.
The victory is won,
And the curse is finally undone.
Though evil and darkness may try and try,
Jesus is the proof true heroes never die.
A saint dies so others may live.
The King is alive.

Matthew 28:1-4
"After the Sabbath, at dawn on the first day of
the week, Mary Magdalene and the other Mary
went to look at the tomb.
There was a violent earthquake, for an angel of
the Lord came down from heaven and, going to
the tomb, rolled back the stone and sat on it. His
appearance was like lightning, and his clothes
were white as snow. The guards were so afraid
of him that they shook and became like dead
men."

Luke 20:37-38

" 'But in the account of the burning bush, even
Moses showed that the dead rise, for he calls the
Lord 'the God of Abraham, and the God of
Isaac, and the God of Jacob.' He is not the God
of the dead, but of the living, for to him all are
alive.' "

κλέος κια νόστος

I'm on the return journey, ready to finally sail
home.
Just like there's no land like Ithaca,
There is no place like Florida, being there with
friends and family.

It was time to set sail, go to war, and go roam.
The past had been grand, but now I had to
envision a
Future. No telling, when I set foot on the sand,
what I would see.
Even when I left, I knew I would be ready at any
time, to sail home.

I was gone for what felt like a millennia,
It wasn't what I expected, but a war and an epic
odyssey.
Now I press on, but my bow is always cutting
the sea foam.
I'm returning to Florida, like the Mastermind
returning to Ithaca.

Though I had many victories, the last two years
felt like fighting the sea.
In the tempest I learned to embrace my Savior
more, and I found shalom.

God, while Neptune was against me, I'm sure
glad I was with ya.
Now I return for glory and homecoming, friends
and family.

I made the return journey. I finally made it
home.
Just like for him it was a struggle to return to
Ithaca,
It was my odyssey to get back to Florida, with
friends and family.

John 20:15-18
"He asked her, 'Woman, why are you crying?
Who is it you are looking for?'

Thinking he was the gardener, she said, 'Sir, if
you have carried him away, tell me where you
have put him, and I will get him.'
Jesus said to her, 'Mary.'

She turned toward him and cried out in Aramaic,
'Rabboni!' (which means "Teacher").

Jesus said, 'Do not hold on to me, for I have not
yet ascended to the Father. Go instead to my
brothers and tell them, 'I am ascending to my
Father and your Father, to my God and your
God.'

Mary Magdalene went to the disciples with the news: 'I have seen the Lord!' And she told them that he had said these things to her."

Sound of Waves

I can see the next dune before me,
But I can't see into the distance.
The fog enshrouds us in mystery
So we return to the boats, out of habit,
Like a trance.
Just like before our lives were changed,
We lower the nets,
But a journey like ours, no one forgets.

Even still the sound of waves
Unceasing reminds me.
Though the struggle is hard, God's power is
more
Powerful than the tempest.
His love is more vast than the sea.
It's reassuring, that God's thoughts towards me,
Outnumber the grains of sand on the shore.

The night grows long and cold.
As we wait for the break of day,
It's only by the stars we find our way.
Feels like the days before we followed,
Those days of old.
The moon shines just enough to illuminate
Our empty nets.
I remember back to when He and I first met,

But now, we fish and fish, and wait.

Though the night is long,
The moon gives us proof,
Somewhere, the sun still shines on.
When hope is feeling aloof,
The stars remind me of God's promise
To our father.
Looking out across the sea,
I remember walking on the water.

Now the fog is lifting,
As the winds are shifting,
And a man is standing by the water,
Waiting on the shore.
"On your right," he calls out.
And the catch we pull up,
Is more than we could barter for.
"It's the Lord!" John shouts.
I had my doubts before
But now I know,
Love is standing on the shore.

So when our lives are filled with strife,
And our souls weighed down with hiraeth,
The longing for a home we've never been to,
But we still somehow miss,
Hang on to the promise,
Look to the stars,

In this novalunosis,
That one day we will be in His arms
The arms of the Father, in perfect bliss.

John 21: 9-11, 17
"When they landed, they saw a fire of burning
coals there with fish on it, and some bread.

Jesus said to them, 'Bring some of the fish you
have just caught.' So Simon Peter climbed back
into the boat and dragged the net ashore. It was
full of large fish, 153, but even with so many the
net was not torn.

The third time he said to him, "Simon son of
John, do you love me?"

Peter was hurt because Jesus asked him the third
time, "Do you love me?" He said, "Lord, you
know all things; you know that I love you."

Jesus said, "Feed my sheep."

Matthew 28:18-20
"Then Jesus came to them and said, 'All
authority in heaven and on earth has been given
to me. Therefore go and make disciples of all
nations, baptizing them in the name of the Father
and of the Son and of the Holy Spirit, and

teaching them to obey everything I have commanded you. And surely I am with you always, to the very end of the age.' "

John 21:25
"Jesus did many other things as well. If every one of them were written down, I suppose that even the whole world would not have room for the books that would be written."